A Provisional Map of the Lost Continent

M000087762

POETS OUT LOUD

Elisabeth Frost, *series editor*

A Provisional Map
of the Lost Continent

Poems

Gregory Mahrer

Fordham University Press   New York   2016

Copyright © 2016 Fordham University Press

All rights reserved. No part of this publication
may be reproduced, stored in a retrieval system,
or transmitted in any form or by any means—
electronic, mechanical, photocopy, recording, or any
other—except for brief quotations in printed reviews,
without the prior permission of the publisher.

Fordham University Press has no responsibility for
the persistence or accuracy of URLs for external
or third-party Internet websites referred to in this
publication and does not guarantee that any content
on such websites is, or will remain, accurate or
appropriate.

Interior monotypes are by Harry Frank: page xii,
"Neap Tide"; page 18, "Remnants" (detail); page 36,
"The Laguna." Harryfrank.com.

Fordham University Press also publishes its books
in a variety of electronic formats. Some content that
appears in print may not be available in electronic
books.

Visit us online at www.fordhampress.com.

Library of Congress Cataloging-in-Publication Data

Mahrer, Gregory.
 [Poems. Selections]
 A provisional map of the lost continent : poems /
Gregory Mahrer.
     pages cm. — (Poets out loud)
 ISBN 978-0-8232-7115-3 (pbk. : alk. paper)
 I. Title.
PS3613.A349338A6 2016
811'.6—dc23

                                    2015032621

Printed in the United States of America

18 17 16   5 4 3 2 1

First edition

Contents

III

Foreword *John Yau*

Who is the figure that has used words to "draw" *A Provisional Map of the Lost Continent*? Is it the poet, Gregory Mahrer, his alter ego or dramatis personae? A clue can be found near the beginning of the first poem, "Red City": "We searched inside the *throats of thirteen swallows.*" In "swallows" I hear a muffled cry, a longing to be heard. It is this longing—in registers embracing the inchoate, the charged and the eloquent—that Mahrer hears and voices.

Who is this "we"? Whom is the poet speaking for, the reader might ask? The same perspicacious reader might also ask, Who or what is speaking through the poet?

Behind these questions looms the poem's opening line: "*Go toward the red city* they said."

Are these voices heard in a dream? Are they voices of those who made the artifacts and built the now crumbling walls? Are we part of an army of conquistadors looking for the fabled city of El Dorado? Are we on Mars with John Carter? Are we on an archaeological dig? Or are "we" the barbarians that C. P. Cavafy warned his readers about? So many questions, so much to consider. Such is the density of everyday life, and of history stretching back to the Pleistocene, all of it alive. *A Provisional Map of the Lost Continent* is a world teeming with multitudes.

In the opening poem, "Red City," of this marvelous book, Gregory Mahrer's use of pronouns shifts from "they" and "we" to "the muzzled pronoun that is I." In this shift, which spans centuries and civilizations, the poet travels with a keen eye toward "the numbered vacancy" of those civilizations that preceded us, as well as an acute sensitivity to the phenomenological: "Is it the seed's architecture that is eternal/ or its discarded carapace?"

What does it mean to be "a guest among small swarms of winged insects"?

At times, while reading this book, I thought Mahrer's "we" to be the voice (and voices) of all our ancestors, those whose cities and artifacts we have discovered, and those about whom we know nothing. And in these cities, you might be "a street vendor" or "a blacksmith." At other times, I could not distinguish between the "I" of the poem and "the shuttered window," as both speak in the same insistent whisper. There is a quiet urgency running through this book that animates each word, each step in the journey.

If this is a book about writing a book, or drawing a "provisional map," what do you do when "the narrative breaks off"? What do you do with "the crushed spectacles/ of a minor poet?" "The narrator," Mahrer tells us, "does not specify:/ It could be Madrid in '37, Antigua in late May" . . .

What can we learn from all the artifacts that we have gathered? What will be our contribution to this scattered archive? *A Provisional Map of the Lost Continent* is haunting. Extinction, it suggests, is inevitable.

At times, the voice of these poems is oracular:

> Perhaps everything will be made clear
> when the power returns, when the shining city
>
> rises from its careless rubble and no one speaks
> of Sumeria, or the sky's museum of open graves—

This is a book of fables, facts, and prophecies, about time past, the present, and the future bearing down upon us.

This is a book that belongs on the same shelf with Jorge Luis Borges and Henri Michaux.

It is a book in which we hear a "distant tatter of songs."

Gregory Mahrer, who listens carefully to the voices inside him and does not reject the reports they bring him, full of terrifying and beautiful music, wrote this wise and beautiful book. We would be remiss not to listen to what he has come to tell us.

Acknowledgments

Grateful acknowledgment is made to the editors of the following journals, in which these poems first appeared:

Colorado Review: "Travelogue"
Crazyhorse: "Franciscan Mélange," "Defenestration"
Fourteen Hills: "Drift," "Fable"
Green Mountains Review: "Red City," "Camera Obscura," "Dinner Guests," "Blackout"
Hayden's Ferry Review: "Hinterland"
Indiana Review: "Age of Glass"
New England Review: "Afterlife"
Rhino: "Ciudad de las Manos"
Spillway: "An Unaddressed Envelope Fills with Snow," "En Las Calles de Borges," "Refrain"
Volt: "Alternation of Flight and Perching"

Thanks to the Monday Night Writers group (Kathleen Winter, Carol Lundberg, Phyllis Meshulam, John Johnson, Iris Dunkle, and Jodi Hottel) for enduring, and assisting with early drafts of, many of the poems found here—in particular Kathleen for her encouragement and gentle prodding about submissions. I'd also like to honor the memory of group member Paula Koneazny, whose wisdom and generosity helped make these poems better.

Thanks also to Francesca Bell for broadening my sense of a poetic life, Glenn James and Maya Khosla for being early and careful readers, Susan Terris for championing my work, and Elisabeth Frost and John Yau for choosing the collection. To my family, in particular Madeline, Julian, and Gillian. To Lisa Gluskin Stonestreet and David St. John for their keen editorial eyes and encouragement when it was needed most. And to Brenda Hillman for her longstanding belief in my work, and for showing me another way through.

Thus I found myself in a strange country. This Paraguay is not the Paraguay that exists on our maps. It is not to be found on the continent, South America; it is not a political subdivision of that continent, with a population of 2,161,000 and a capital city Ausuncíon. This Paraguay exists elsewhere.

—DONALD BARTHELME, "PARAGUAY"

I

Red City

Go toward the red city they said

        and we went to where the ground

      rose up against the stubborn dark of noon.

Find where the sevens are sown.

          We searched inside *the throats of thirteen swallows.*

What we heard   (that everything growing here

      vined toward *theoretical blue*) proved false.

The minutes continued to fall about our sloping shoulders

    cuffing our ears like iron kisses.

In the appended churchyard

             we traipsed arm in fist

      among the twitch and lurch of sprung earth

         green camouflaging green.

The elders must have known

      the city was on fire when they loosed vandals

        from their armoires.

   Where the library once stood,

        fragments of the twelve known plotlines,

          a few loose vowels to take the measure of what was lost.

From here it was a short jaunt to the confessional,

        but the booths were full and besides

    what was there to confess other than the same tattered narrative:

Once I resided among kettlefish and barricades, etc.etc.

   Thinking back, salt was too good for us.Pumice and ash

        will register the silhouettes of our fabulous lives—

small squalls wrapped in papier-mâché,

      the muzzled pronoun that is I.

Studies (Graphite and Pollen)

What was once a small civilization
comes to us as numbered vacancy—

fragment of bowl and pestle, encampment
of ambered husk. But what of the windpipe,

the clavicle? Even a child's clay top
outlasts childhood by a millennium or two.

Is it the seed's architecture that is eternal
or its discarded carapace?

What is the artifact of *veer*? Of *slant*?
Of *extinction*? Stranded between

what is occluded and what has elapsed—
the felicities of the eloping landscape.

Drift

I am a guest among small swarms of winged insects
their vernacular rough against my skin.

I have left the long cursive of your body
to stroll the Miocenian grasslands, skittery

in the powdery light.One epoch is dying into another—
you can hear the buzzing against the glisten,

stars wheeling in a broken halo.Suddenly all I want
is to become aquatic, to return

to that watery place where drift is a form of propulsion,
and we little more than bell and tentacle—

votive shudders gathering in the outer precincts,
our future tiny and invertebrate.

Ciudad de Oro

Washed against other alluvial bodies
we waited centuries for the rains to end.
North was still beyond our reach.
South had not yet been assigned a star.
Our muskets remained as invisible

as hooves buried deep in the bodies of whales.
We crossed a series of valleys
still short of the interior.
We were left to wonder what if anything
could be built of sturdier air.

Navigation requires a backward glance
but our helmets were heavy as we approached the capital.
No matter the vector, we remained
at the outskirts. Much of the city was underwater,
a gush of pale letters and torn urns.

To a man we felt the bruise of place
missing its address: the far districts strung together
by imagined filaments, broken and hungry horses
sinking beneath a column of air.
What voices remained read as an iambic shout.

It was like sifting through swans and ashes
for the one bitter penny, finding several—
the spill of moonlight was that close upon us.
We could still feel the places in our bodies
where the Pleistocene had laid down its long
ribbons of mud.

In the unsettled light we made camp and set about
perfecting the maps. Within their gilded borders:
the world we had left behind, only wider
at the isthmuses and subject to revision.

Itinerary of Fire

The air must have been thick with insects and smoke:
    neither breathable nor nameable, a series

    of black guesses that enters the lungs.

We are directed to follow the slope of the body
    down through its divergent calamities:
        one that ends in ash, another iron.

Remember how the skin gathered around the milky hollows
of her knees?

    Had we been given a simpler itinerary
    we might have come to a different door.

In the half-open room a thin drift of flour covers the table.
    Olives, still vatted and brined, await each guest.

We are not yet hollow, unweighted.

In the reprieve let us count the stars as they fall
through a slipknot of sky, crouch as though entering
    a second earth
    wider and more radiant than the first.

Hinterland

There was a civic place I had to pass through
on my way to the thin longitudes of marshland and spire.
Only now does the sun confide

its fractured alliance with the hourglass.Tell me more
than I can possibly disclose.Tell me the cost of lying low
while the canals run red with starlight.

Put down your knife and walk with me beyond the drifting cisterns.
Of the three names for drowning in brackish water
and the one enduring word for exile, which shall I choose?

There is no longer a *twice* to go back to.Stay with me
in the weak sunlight of old empires—that adjacent world
where everything, even extinction, is still waiting to be invented.

Franciscan Mélange

Tell me what you know of the slope of rust in sag ponds,
fracture in the volition of stream beds.

The comma's slow knife.

Don't speak yet.It is imperative we not speak
the notspeak spoken here.

(We are brought into smaller and smaller rooms.)

In an act of subduction, the Pacific Plate
slips beneath the North American.

A part of the diagrammed sentence drifts south.
Learn to love "no," its fallen shape
a glacial lake cut from its cloud.

We are not yet the subject, not range or outcropping.

If this tango is to last, then *tengo que tener prisa*:
hurry to where the mixing is.

Blackout

Other guests speak from behind their hands.
Are they holding stolen artifacts under their coats?

Each ruined stair seems pillaged
from the city's older levels.

Singed devices sing for the lost socket—
the smoke alarm, the toaster, the broken statuary.

None of us can loosen the shrouds of ice
or remember the circumstances of our arrival.

If the ramparts are unassailable, why this swarm
of tremors, this dependence on soft tissue?

Perhaps everything will be made clear
when the power returns, when the shining city

rises from its careless rubble and no one speaks
of Sumeria, or the sky's museum of open graves—

Travelogue

Outside the frame, shimmer wants our attention—
an inland sea, a high window, the crushed spectacles
of a minor poet. The narrator does not specify:
It could be Madrid in '37, Antigua in late May...

An urgency curls the day's image
which floats above us in the filmy smoke.
Fluent in betrayal, the translator (a village priest)
has locked up every vowel.

Once I was instructed to hide myself
in an underground empire of mason jars and boots.
None of us knew then which of our lives we should keep
or which country might desire our excellent services.

If only my father had raised his voice,
or set paper saints ablaze in foreign districts—

Who am I if not the shuttered window?
I learn to sleep in separate frames, obedient
to the smallest of vistas.

When I say *blood orange* I mean the fidelity of sunflowers,
story the distance between sill and toppled chair.

The Age of Glass

A window's deepest frequency must remember
something of sand, the soft angle of warm rain.
I did not want to wake in this age.I would have
preferred the age before the age of glass.
I was happier in the time of ice and knives.
Happier still in the tumble-bright sea.
No readable surface, swirl of spilled ink,
the transparencies of water uncontested.

I could have moved invisibly
in an underground of incipient rivers.
As for moons I have seen them drown in barrels.

All those years devoted to the practice
of becoming smooth, a swarm of small
mouths nested just under the skin,
more strata than sky.

Whiteout

Even the trees are wired

        for sound

           though the falling snow   muzzles everything:

    the inscription on the page,

           footnotes, marginalia,

the tremor the hand makes

      as it slays another word.

The sun too is dying. Imagine

        a grammar—made

           of silences, a blotted sky,

the assassin's random knife.

       In place of the alphabet,

a small government stipend.

What is erased is done to protect

          certain public buildings.

    Fewer and fewer letters available

        not at liberty to discuss . . .

Let me just say

    how much I love

the widening   blankness,

     the corrected drafts and galleys

     love the trees of the capital,

         their snowy silence,

the empty page,

the many empty pages

somersaulting

across unsparrowed winter lawns.

An Unaddressed Envelope Fills with Snow

The white margin at the edge of white.

Every wind has died to a flutter: the north wind, the Coho, wind of vespers
$$\text{and of mourning}—$$

       Clouds of small wings settle in the grainy confection
       of the village floor,

the rooms of the sky empty their sullen ice.

       In the clearing the pitching post of the sun throws its light
       over the cairn.

There the narrative breaks off. There the cadence turns white and waits.

       A moment to sleep off what it is that has caught in us—
       deathstar and feverbranch rubble of pen and wristbone

       welt of blue across the horizon.

Memory is too much in the world, and us barely held in its weave.

Turn the page dear diarist plunge into deep and trackless snow.

Write: What is the circumference of white?

             Write: Take us as you find us—

              famished and vanishing.

Alternation of Flight and Perching

Every unwritten letter reveals an open field.
Stamps still carry the scent of foreign capitals.
An unfinished draft unsettles the air a second time.

Who knew what stillness wanted for us?

I am no longer a surplus of quill and ink,
not even a body really,
spinning forever in summer's heat.

I did not mean to unravel so completely
to fall prey to wind's ambush—

a creature who mistakes cloud
for predator, delay for the refuge
of branch and leaf.

Plummet too is a form of rest.

II

Fable

You are taken by sleep
into woods blue as the roped hands
that divide the evening.
Beyond the knot of trees
pale dwellings relinquish
their cuffed heat.
Every unuttered phrase
hangs in the throat like a hex—
sodden den, fretted rook, strangled lyre.
There is no noon, only undertow.
Swim to the surface. Bring scissors
and wax. Make a bigger fire.
Wolves will take you in. Twine
will be your undoing.

Refrain

Before a plan could be formalized a town appeared—

      calamity of streets, dogs barking backwards
      and a general washing of hands that led to more washing

then something vaguely political like air balloons

                         barricades

and rumors of public weather.

Gasoline ran the avenues and word was that soon there would be music
and everywhere a humming or a clearing of throats

              as if what was prophesied was finally

                     upon us.

So we hitched up our gabardines, grabbed the nearest oboist

     looking for the precise angle of entry.

                  What we heard was a distant tatter of songs

arranged as a march, the loose syntax of warm rain bees fuzzy with jazz
           nuzzling the river azaleas.

All along we had wanted the next thing

      and now that it was almost here
      our attention turned to the waitress's narration

of our town's architecture its fallen porticos and maze of rambling rooms.

It made us want to sleep in separate beds coddled by various unsponsored silences

        so that nothing could disturb the popular music playing inside

us,

      nothing could disturb the music inside.

Under: Variations

1.

In a yellow blaze of streets
I was transfixed by a spectacle of undetermined geometry
as if there were still a village beneath the city,
a haberdashery of vials
rising up in glassy octaves.

2.

By *dark nap* you could have meant:
• a bridge between underground settlements
• the substitution of veil for soul
• any stranded thing hiding under its interrogator.

3.

A citizenry under duress wears its indentations
like a crown or breathing apparatus. A shape
it cannot occupy. Lantern, ghost, circle, key.

4.

The burning city is always wider than its perimeter.
A bruise of shadow and angle—a heft
that refuses our leverage only
because it is weightless.

Ciudad de Plata

We entered the city through a system
of limestone cisterns, then secreted ourselves
among the granaries.We knew how to hide
in the manner of stones, but hadn't considered
the lunar eclipse, or the effects of swollen limbs.

Guards had been positioned around the zocalo,
clotted near its atrium.We intended to appropriate
their silk robes, to slip between sleep and sleeve
before the first bright hour.The quicksilver entrails
were difficult to decipher under the moon.

Should we have lowered the ladders,
or continued our ascent? The wind from the east
carried the scent of hibiscus and blood—
a locust wind, some said, sure to disturb the river
and its tattered aqueducts.

Neglecting our compact, we tried out salutations—
as imperative, as subjunctive, as anthem.
We preferred jars of silver to the swelter of welts'
guttural clicks.And still a maze of aviaries
anticipated our every move.

The towers swayed with vertigo.
Below us palanquins moved through fields
of corn and aloe, toward the seven distant climates.
Pressing our advantage, we set fire to the storerooms.
Smoke filled the roads.

But for their hunger, we would have settled among them,
or so we told ourselves in the years to come.
Bathed in their scented waters.Instead we fed them silver
and they died, one by one, each wingless god
shining from within its luminescent cage.

Vacancy

When entering the courtyard, the trick
is not to be undone by the leveling

of field and sky.

Loose birds renovate old shadow lines—

the house suddenly nocturnal
in the way a lampshade is nocturnal.

There will be insomnia

(a sonata goes off in the bed)

the unknown stories perched overhead . . .

Empty chairs preside over the hybrid space
of vestibule and drawing room—

fallen chandeliers lit by their own windowless trembling.

Behind the scrim of underbrush,

a seething proximity:
crumpled balustrade, pried latch.

Once a tribe, then a tribulation
finally a branch

scraping against glass.

Surely someone will answer—
one name culled,

then culled again.

Chimera

What is buried in the blood releases itself a little at a time,
in bouts of euphoria or gout.I was a street vendor once as now

I am a blacksmith working within a cabal of embers.
From a stable of only two ponies I made all the shapes

I was to become, left them to float like straw
above the lanterned cities.

I no longer seek to still the music of the date merchants or drag
my one rebellious foot behind me like fresh kill.

Whenever possible I carry shade with me, offer it oranges
behind the secret compact of my sleeve.

Not yet equal to thrush or serpent
I constructed a boat of loose willow

and pushed out into the wider stream.
As was the custom I cut away the sails at the meridians

tracing circles in the air with my one good lantern.
I intended to be a storm of cormorants

a sunken riverbed a palomino at dusk.
Unrehearsed colors signaling across the horizon's fold.

Flurry

Snow is falling through the broken carapace of the city.
Having lost their hover, bridges and canopies practice impermanence.

With every collapsed perpendicular the fettered world
grows more fragile, an accretion of woolen weather and yellow boots.

Once a hat carried to the far end of a life was roughly equivalent
to that series of rooms from which children or secret ledgers issue.

Now the question your life turns on can hardly be spoken.
Adjacent to the day, a soft thrum of candles leverages the dusk.

In this version, eternity fills with the discarded scribbles of clerks:
an avalanche of integers trapped in each glass tower.

En Las Calles de Borges

Between street corners you held his breath
in two black notebooks, a confluence of amble and collide.

In one example you are seated on a park bench in Plaza San Martín.
Who did you imagine would enter by cart and who by horseback?

Never mind that the voice over the phone repeats that your number
is theoretically impossible. Or that Borges' map of the city is based on a forged original.

A companion was needed, a summary of atria and courtyard.
The soffited eye dreams the circumference of a stranger's glance.

That the phone continues to ring inside a cabinet
is the receiver's unkept secret. Now there are two hemispheres to consider.

Could you, Borges asks, have invented the words for mullion and transom?
Could you stand in their shadows just a moment longer?

Inquest at Century's End

Outside the cordon, a storm of lit trees.
A man with a cane walks from one century to the next.
Where a tower gathers the shoreline westward

the lake has been swept clean. At the inquest
much is made of the hat; less of the stricken shadow,
thrown voice, empty tin box.

The scene is an alloy of other scenes
as the body is a composite of ribboned hair
and narrow stairwell, serpent and hasp.

We pretend not to notice that the bird at the window
is the same one we find lifeless on the doorstep.
Each moment carries extinction in its mouth.

Among the numbered miscellany
we are not yet grazed by the examiner's eye,
not yet trapped between the shuttered greenhouse

and the turned ankle. The tower slips
beneath two surfaces at once. Bring a ladder
someone shouts from behind the shrubbery.

One by one we clamber down.

Empty Square, Twilight

The day is down to an ember
though its hum is endless, its thefts legendary.
Three times I have changed the locks

but I remain a public space.
At the limit of my range I circle back
to find half-remembered interiors—

caskets toppled one against another,
a yellow bird singing in repeating grids
of commerce and consumption.

Can you hear the hurry in its branches
hear its plea light up then empty out?
In every window a bright face blooms

as if awaiting what—spectacle's catastrophe,
the rounding up of suspicious apparel?
Now begins the return journey,

the one without the confectioner.

Corner Plot

Studies are made but stop short of inference—
cursive that bends around borders without igniting the edges.

The important instructions are not written out,
choices pared down to overhang and windbreak,

a plot more elegiac than funereal. Small practices are maintained:
twirled thumbs, tugged earlobe.

Already, the fallen sill has begun to cancel the house
even as the woods remain trapped in glass.

To the rumpled meadow condolences are offered, a green thread
worn to brown. If it were a book, it might be said that it was much loved.

An assembly of trees leans in listening for a path, a way grown
fainter with each rewriting. Corrupted shadows lengthen

to include the water tower, the corrugated fields.
The house adrift: an animal, almost human, turned inside out.

Raft

Now that the sea is rising who will pay attention
to the rescission of gravity—a gust of seagulls

moves out over water mimicking the storm's funnel—
or interrogations begun with velvet gloves about the throat?

Once hands were spoons joining water to water, then knives
dividing sand from stone. Small flightless birds. In the banded light

the gulls have become horizon, the narrowing waters a duplicate sky.
Who foresaw the coming iodine solitudes—redacted species signaling

from the lowlands, lives circled by winged ghosts:
no branch or hillock on which to roost.

Verge

It was, for all its heft, a crooked piece of blue

                and we little more than bent
silhouettes outlined in chalk.I traced a signature across the sand,

                     my hand barely recognizable.

Unspun from its orbit a derelict

              moon had settled like an amber eye.

    You could feel a whisper   under the air as if something

      had been dishonored a green verge that could not be traversed.

Elsewhere elegant guests settled down in their false sobriety

                  tremulous before a fungible god.

The radiant assassin sorts casaba melons in the scant shade of an elephant tree.

      I scribble this sentence in the lobby's antechamber.

    It is a gun that won't go off.

      Who will play the guillotine, the noose, the garrote?

Next time neither red nor black.

      Better a missing face than death

          riding up with the visage of a banker.

Colony

If we are of one mind how to understand the separate fealties

of kindle and hasten.

Beyond this fervent tether

objects unmoored in a pulse of dark matter   flow without a sleeve.

One tires of the self-canceling phrase: the flash of no vacancy

in the desert night

               the leafy voice of god.

What comes down to us is chalky and largely unfathered.
It is all we talk about as we shift in our splendor.

That and the line of dwellings listing toward pilgrimage.

The status of the hive has changed:

Birds stray from their compass   salmon tastes of the wrong silt.

Shoes grow heavy in the field.

We make a vow to gaze skyward more often
but look away the moment we start to ravel

at the edge of so much revocable wilderness.

III

Understory

We enter into the woods as if the first
to be overcome by a delirium of trees.
In the close air little erasures of time:
a coupling of blue and found, eye and gone.
Then the understory ticks up.

Who had prepared the way back better than I?
Satchel of marbles, seed packet, string.
I wasn't made for sunlessness
but neither was I made for the salt plain
or the water wheel.

It is not enough to understand the scant wind,
the fraying on a low branch.There will be
blood on the ground,
the blunt insects.
Where then the safe hollow of down?

Beyond the declarations of paper
or the prurience of strung birds
our disappearance will be as unheralded
as the sleep of trees,
as irreversible as inbreath and outcast.

A Provisional Map of the Lost Continent

There were two of us then,
errant Magellans, the sea
or its rumor at our backs.

Sand was the language we spoke:
I of delay, you of circumnavigation.
Where we should have been fluent
only dashes and stops.

We had wanted to be the first to discover
the lost republic of *vosotros*.

You asked
Who can slow the velocity of sleep
or *salt's migration?*

We had yet to speak of entropy's majesty
whether it was a circuit
of high vicissitudes we were entering
or oxidation's weave.

Circumference is not a perfect circle.

When you spoke of seabirds
a fog moved through you.
For a long time description
failed to account for array or cluster.

(We appear in patches, flutter.)

Sail is not hull but neither is it wave.

A map of the wind perhaps, a chain of words.
An archipelago of blue and yellow birds.

Beneath this sea is there no other?
The latitudes of amber
release their languid thefts.
A ghost continent hurries toward its shade

Ciudad de las Manos

Where the landscape fell away
fracture became a kind of fastening.
We gave it a name and set about building a city there.

The plan was to begin with the template
of the body, to trace the length of a foot,
the width of a finger. The distance of a step.

We considered solitude, how it too
might have a locus. But *to span* insisted on
merge, on the close angle.

Charts never imagined the steep particularity
of narrow streets, the plague of small birds
that swooped in from bluer climes.

Some of us had wanted to codify the interval
between hand and eye, but the interiors
were already withdrawing from our reach.

We planted the mango's oval seed between rafts of adobe,
waited for its green imperative. It was
more and more difficult to imagine

the imprimatur of the hand, the arc of a public square.
And the wind, around which everything had been wound,
started to uncoil.

We had neglected in the early two-chambered light to invent
more than one sun and now it was falling once and for all
beyond the spires of our city,

its yellow fruit everywhere
and everywhere uneaten.

Dinner Guests

Your blue scent,
the bare knees of our first kiss
strung up in a wind of straight-backed chairs.

Where once there was meadow and fir
stands a small grove of Presbyterians—
a disturbance of thistle and leaf.

Beneath your hand an oracle of clouds.
the leap of tides, every summer fish.

Meanwhile the children under the table
invent a city of steeples and nooses.

Birds shabbily dressed as dinner guests
gather in the canopy, each searching
for the bright seed of the larynx.
A benediction of beaks,

and we a heresy of wings.

Ideograph

We learned of tremors in the field, vagrancy
in the written tongue. In that season the grammarian's pen
rode us through a series of streets—then, breathless,
through longer and longer rooms.

In the last, a man caught in translation set fire
to two sets of forbidden letters.

I come from a large family (he might have said)
organized around a single vowel. No one
knows its sound but on paper it is represented
by a solitary dot of ink.

The technique is quite simple—a few thrown
breaths followed by a series of gestural forays—
but its effect is rather like riding
bareback through sawgrass.

Later when we came to the burning house
we mistook the man outside for the man inside.
It was autumn and all of our failures were there,
the occluded months irreconcilable.

What we heard was a rushing in every direction
as if the figure for obstacle were the same as that for door.
What we heard were the endless unlockings
of clasp and release.

Icelandia

We cannot stop looking at the overturned
nest, its mosaic of broken shells.

If we were to homestead here
might we begin with candle and claw?

I'm an insomniac asleep in the icebox,
a lone polar bear adrift on a raft of ice.

You love the world best
when it sleeps. Less when it crawls back to you.

The hand that bites, the smile that corners a room.
Winter comes early to these parts. The fingers especially.

Cover me in a garment that is warm-blooded, hooded.
Bludgeon the tundra into units of heat.

A Sequence of Knots

A curfew of satin and wool shackles the evening.

There is no *further* that does not also suggest contraction.

Small birds shape the darkening field   which burns from the inside.

What is adjacent to the visible   is visible

and it is there   the amorous eye has fled:

illicit, occult, a flutter without a perch.

An apostrophe awaiting possession.

Fandango

Into the tremble we twirled and leapt, fandangoed noon till night.

Everything was wrong
the bog grass bent into the wind
birds flew backward into the teeth of predators
the air smelled of fly ash and homicide.

What is kindled here slips under fence lines
crossing from description into tremor.
Panic as a shuffled chronology:
first the death of stars then the passerine nocturnes.

Nature is a foolish, useless thing.
Smoke will clear the trees of nests,
burnish the grasslands.In the garlanded clearing
a dirge nestles against his bride.

Blurred sky, what can you offer now?
It was always going to be a narrow escape.
But now that no one is singing, who will sing
the dark-eyed junko to sleep?

Defenestration

From here I can see the walls of the city,
crowded doorways, the half-life of windows,
a descent that began high in the heavens
and fell through the streets without
anyone turning to look.

The field of action has shifted from the sea
to what has spilled from it; vertebrate,
girdered, silicate, above which
a lone voice, having been thrown
beyond its body's green veldt, now floats.

It might have been your voice
except for its thin height, its half-
cry of a gull torn from its wings,
or a moth perishing
in one of many small suns.

What shatters first is not glass, not
the thrown die of the body.But
every ghost, passing through
reflection and into incalculable air.

As in the Letter O

It was decided he should make a practice of swallowing.
He began with small objects, a ring of smoke, a paper silhouette, the letter O
quickly moving to insomnia, a bright interval, improper nouns.

It was no longer about commerce or long division.
More a state of providence, a partition—beautiful throat, ecumenical mouth—
that wanted to be a bridge.

To be both a body and incorporeal—
floating, slack-jawed outside the frame of the self—
requires a wide network of roots.

As a child he held his breath until seven
wore the long sleeves of desultory Sundays.
To run in one direction for a long while is not biography

nor is it quite a place. A series of descriptions
scudded one against another until
only the shape of incorporation remains.

As in jawbone, as in bowl.

Glossolalia

Loon tongue
        muttertongue
                idiom savant.

Beneath this tongue
        they say
                lies another tongue.

But what of the throat: lingual reed
        tender slide of oboe
                guttural click—

or torso
        flutter of sparrow
                shuttle box?

Wrist glyph
        phoneme of hip
                ibble of lash . . .

What is the saying
        that in the saying
                reveals the underword?

Caress
        the indigestible
                pronoun

Funnel seed
        quill
                shuttle and yarn.

Accident

Something white flies into view

        a movement between parentheses

  tilting at the border of wakefulness.

Upon the fevered glass something brighter

        than obsolescence is tapping.
¿*Adónde va el avión* (in its desperate choreography)?
¿*Qué quiere el viento* (con la barda quebrada)?

A plane's wing smolders at the end of a field.

        I carry water to the edge of its opacity.
        Then the sound of birds begins
        to fill in the torn sky.

Never mind the accidental metonymy   the empty hull against the hill.
  Mind the drift of smoke, the cry being prepared behind the gusseted trees.

The tear is the voice not yet fragmented in the telling:

  the smalling world redolent of gasoline and gin

        a parachute drifting by unattended—things (parenthetical)

  to be unpacked in the redrawn
  lineage of the aftermath.

Camera Obscura

By day the room holds almost pure image—

        the cellist in the park with her inverted bow

               and wilted pearls.

    Later a pair of swans

        felled by the pond's thin blade.

      More intimate than the body's address

is image unpinned

               from its sound.

        Two inclinations:

To drift to the bottom of the room   an abandoned tourniquet of white roses

      or linger in the weak light of perpetual evening.

     Did you choose the paler less blemished world,

        for its soft iteration of dappled acetate?

Or did you, like me, wish to protect the eye

        from the scene's original amplitude?

The narrow boulevard with its   phalanx of trees

      less fixed with every passing shadow.

      As if we were somehow both the camera and the film

the durations of dislocated light   measured out in hues just before the screen

vanishes or the aperture darkens.

     How many exits remain to us

        now that the accidental theater is both

   prism and refuge?   The dilutions have been calming but not more than

    the forged plurals of dark.

If only I were so composed.   I could have made

of the room

a better instrument.

All along I have lived for the windfall of imperfect

translations but like you

would have settled for the simple radiance

of pearls.

Apprenticeship

Here are my mimeographed reports

Speech seeks the tender hollow of an ear but will settle for any of the blue atmospheres

The neighbor's dog easily attends to several silences at once but I must work
to retrieve the simplest of sounds

The peach fallen from its espaliered perch   unfinished dusk

How long we have followed along the fretted surface noted its beauty
from our separate principalities

Once I traced a series of interruptions to the end of the line.I found
no comfort there—only a scratched record playing out its grooves

I have lived a long time between utterances   I have been an apprentice
to many weathers   I have tried to love the small quiet of the present tense

to find this   faint smudge of ink on my temples the delayed embrace of winter
clothes

Afterlife

We remember the darkness at our backs, the spine of stars.

How each memory was sifted, then offered back to us from the ash of our bodies.

How the night plow spilled its cargo of ice over the curved fields.

Murmur of smoke at the edge of the woods.

A crucible of starlings, open sky.

Now two more suns and the moon smaller by half; at the end of the day, another day.

This is not the heaven we counted on, still so knotted to the blue world.

We remain winter shadows, heat rising from rooftops—

Blade and bee falling endlessly before the scythe of the sun.

POETS OUT LOUD *Prize Winners*

Gregory Mahrer

A Provisional Map of the Lost Continent

Nancy K. Pearson

The Whole by Contemplation of a Single Bone

EDITOR'S PRIZE

Daneen Wardrop

Cyclorama

Terrence Chiusano

On Generation & Corruption

EDITOR'S PRIZE

Sara Michas-Martin

Gray Matter

Peter Streckfus

Errings

EDITOR'S PRIZE

Amy Sara Carroll

Fannie + Freddie: The Sentimentality of Post–9/11 Pornography

Nicolas Hundley
The Revolver in the Hive
EDITOR'S PRIZE

Julie Choffel
The Hello Delay

Michelle Naka Pierce
Continuous Frieze Bordering Red
EDITOR'S PRIZE

Leslie C. Chang
Things That No Longer Delight Me

Amy Catanzano
Multiversal

Darcie Dennigan
Corinna A-Maying the Apocalypse

Karin Gottshall
Crocus

Jean Gallagher
This Minute

Lee Robinson
Hearsay